A Strange Day at the Zoo

Contents

Written by Amanda Brownfeather
Illustrated by Brent Putze

Outside the Zoo

Patrick was in a hurry to get to work. He was an animal keeper at the zoo, and he loved his job.

Patrick sniffed the air. He liked the smell of the zoo.

When he came to the zoo entrance, Patrick looked up. Over the main gate was a big sign. It usually said, *Zoological Park*. But today it said *Zoo   ark*. The middle bit of the sign was missing. Well, not really missing, but hidden.

Patrick couldn't believe his eyes. He stopped. He blinked. It couldn't be true. But it was. Lying along the top of the sign was a hippopotamus! Patrick stared at the hippopotamus and the hippopotamus stared back at Patrick.

"What are you doing up there?" asked Patrick. " How did you get up there?"

The hippo opened its huge mouth and yawned. Out of the corner of his eye, Patrick saw an enormous shape floating through the air. It was another hippo, and this one was flying!

The second hippo landed gently in a tree. It was a big tree, which was a good thing, because hippos are very heavy. The tree wobbled a bit, but the hippo wiggled around and let its legs hang over a branch. It looked so funny that Patrick started to laugh.

The hippos looked hard at Patrick. They did not look very happy.

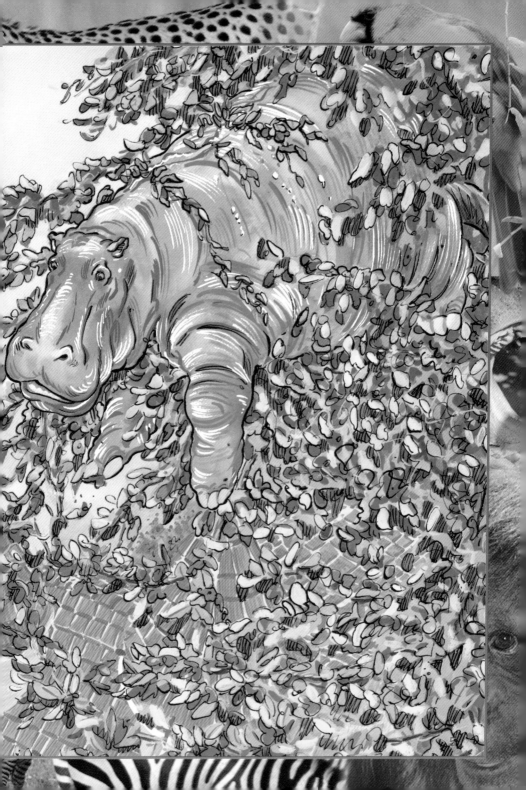

Inside the Zoo

Patrick hurried through the zoo gates. He was feeling excited and a bit worried at the same time.

He came to the giraffe enclosure. No giraffes!

So he went on to the lake, where the seals usually swam. No seals!

But suddenly, three giraffe heads popped out of the water. They had bits of weed twisted around their horns. They looked so funny that Patrick wanted to laugh at them, too. The giraffes' long necks poked up like periscopes on submarines. They stared at Patrick, then slid down under the water and blew bubbles.

"This is all very strange," said Patrick to himself. "I wonder what's happening. Someone must be playing a trick."

He walked around a bend to the flamingos' lake. Usually the flamingos were standing around on one leg. But not today. Today they were with the meerkats. The meerkats were all trying to stand on one leg, but they kept falling over. The flamingos were acting like meerkats. They were pecking the ground, trying to dig burrows. They all looked so funny that Patrick laughed and laughed.

Just then Patrick heard the sound of running feet and Jane, another keeper, came around the bend.

"You won't believe what I've just seen," she puffed. "The lions are acting just like seals. They're balancing balls on their noses and barking."

"There's something very funny going on here," said Patrick. "Did you notice the sign over the main gate?"

"No, I came in by the side entrance. What's wrong with it?" asked Jane.

"Come with me and I'll show you," replied Patrick.

Together they raced to the main gate. The sign still said
Zoo   ark, but now there was another hippo floating
above the sign. This one was small, just a baby. It was
showing off to the others, doing flips and rolls in the air. But
the hippo on the sign just closed its eyes and started
to snore.

"Let's check the rest of the animals," said Patrick.

Animal Antics

The cheetahs were strolling along at a snail's pace, purring loudly, and the turtles were running races with each other. The zebras were swimming and diving.

"These are the strangest animals I've ever seen," said Jane. "Someone *must* be playing a trick."

"Let's go and check out the monkeys," said Patrick.

The monkeys were doing all the usual monkey things. They looked rather pleased with themselves.

"That's a bit odd," said Jane. "They're the only ones who haven't changed. I bet they know something. We'd better keep an eye on them. But first, let's see what the elephants are doing."

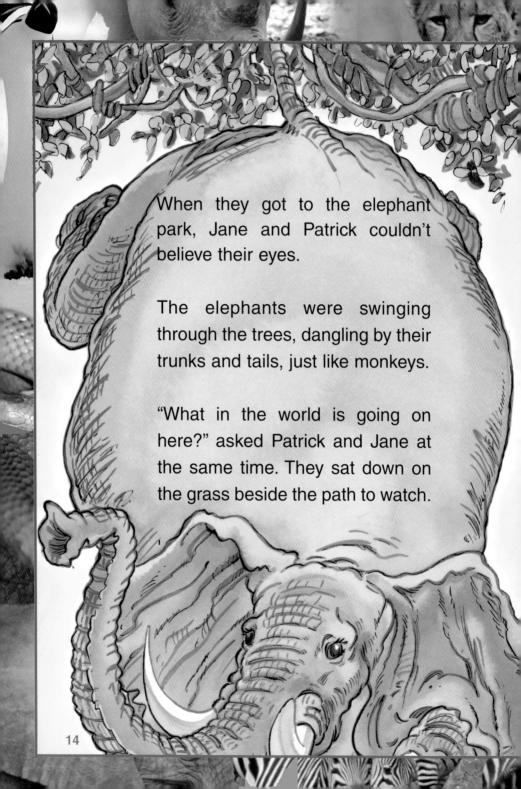

When they got to the elephant park, Jane and Patrick couldn't believe their eyes.

The elephants were swinging through the trees, dangling by their trunks and tails, just like monkeys.

"What in the world is going on here?" asked Patrick and Jane at the same time. They sat down on the grass beside the path to watch.

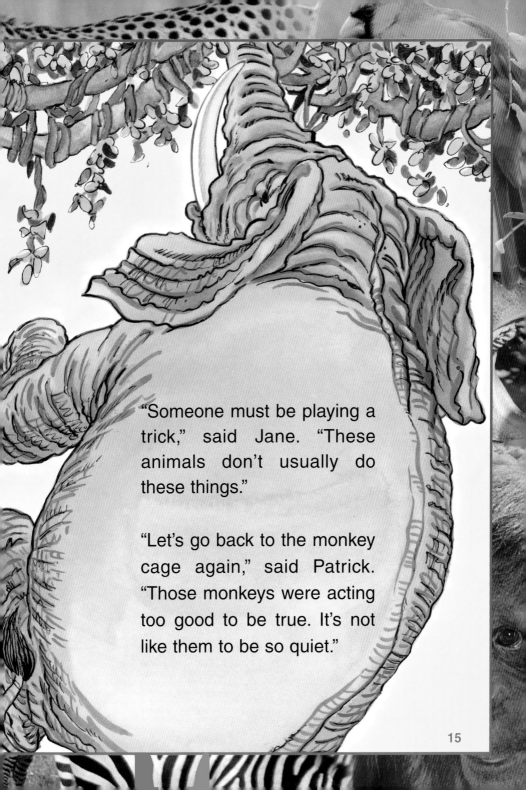

"Someone must be playing a trick," said Jane. "These animals don't usually do these things."

"Let's go back to the monkey cage again," said Patrick. "Those monkeys were acting too good to be true. It's not like them to be so quiet."

Monkey Business

Back at the monkey cage, everything was still normal and quiet. The monkeys sat on branches grooming each other.

The biggest monkey grabbed a banana. He crammed it into his mouth, chewed it, and burped loudly. Then he jumped down close to Patrick and Jane. He had something in his hand.

'What's that monkey holding?" asked Jane.

'I can't see," replied Patrick.

The monkey seemed to grin at them, then he turned his back and jumped back up into the tree.

Something in the Air

"Come on," said Jane to Patrick. "Let's go around the zoo again and see if anything's changed back to normal."

Nothing had. Zebras were sunbathing with their legs in the air. Lions were clapping their front paws and barking. Elephants were still swinging in the trees, and the turtles were chasing the meerkats. Above them, the hippos were doing acrobatics and swooping down to scare the flamingos. It really was very, very strange.

"I think that big monkey knows something," Jane said.

Just then a hippo glided past. Jane and Patrick looked at each other. They were worried. What if the hippos suddenly stopped being able to fly while they were up in the air? They would crash to the ground.

"We must find out what is making all this happen," said Patrick. "We have to get the animals back to normal before one of them gets hurt."

More Monkey Business

Back at the monkey cage, everything was still quiet. The biggest monkey was pretending to sleep, but every now and then he would look down at his hand.

Jane and Patrick decided it was time to find out what was going on, so they went right into the monkey park. The monkeys took no notice of them at all.

Just then, Jane and Patrick heard a strange clicking sound. It was coming from the thing in the big monkey's hand.

"Come on, show us what you're holding, that's a good monkey," Patrick said. But the big monkey just jumped up a tree. Then, just as a turtle raced past and a hippo flew past, Peter and Jane heard the clicks again.

The big monkey chose that moment to swing to another tree. As he grabbed a branch, he slipped and a little box fell from his hand.

start / fast

stop / slow

25

Patrick grabbed the box, and he and Jane hurried out of the monkey park.

"Look at this," Patrick said. "The box has two buttons on top. One button says *start/fast*, and the other one says *stop/slow*."

"There were some children here yesterday," said Jane. "One of them must have dropped it. I heard them talking about an electronics project they were doing at school."

"Let's see if we can make it work," said Patrick, as a turtle came racing past them. He pressed the *stop/slow* button. The turtle slowed down, and then went on its way at its normal speed.

"That's it!" shouted Jane. "Let's try it on the other animals."

Together they raced around the zoo. Every time they saw an animal doing something funny, Patrick pressed the *stop/slow* button until the animal was back to normal.

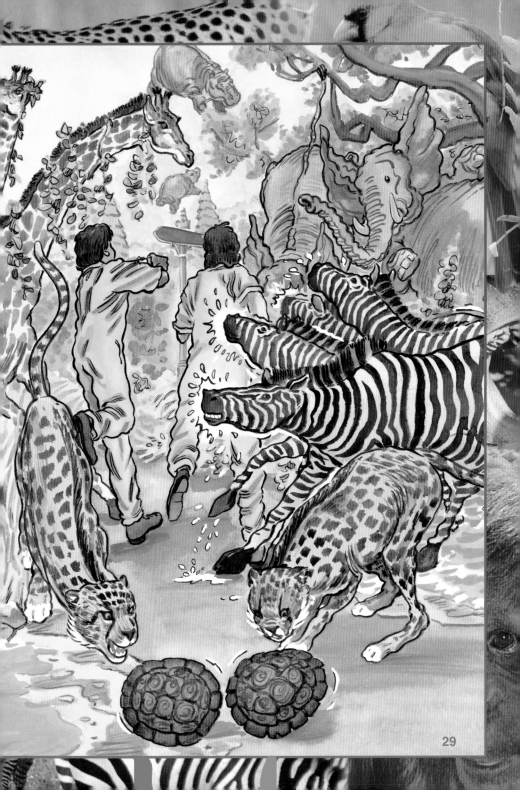

Last of all they came to the hippos.

"I'm really worried about them. I'd hate them to fall," said Patrick.

"Just press the button very slowly," said Jane.

So Patrick pressed the button very, very slowly. Very, very slowly the hippos flew in a line back to the hippo pond and gently slipped into the water.

At last, all the animals were in the right place doing the right things.

As they left the zoo that night, Patrick and Jane looked up at the sign above the entrance. It said *Zoological Park*.

"I hope it will still be like this tomorrow when I come to work," said Patrick. "I've had enough excitement for one week."